AL EAST

BOSTON
RED SOX

RICHARD RAMBECK

Published by Creative Education, Inc.
123 S. Broad Street, Mankato, Minnesota 56001

Art Director, Rita Marshall
Cover and title page design by Virginia Evans
Cover and title page illustration by Rob Day
Type set by FinalCopy Electronic Publishing
Book design by Rita Marshall

Photos by Duomo, Focus on Sports, FPG, National Baseball Library, Bruce Schwartzman, Sportschrome West, UPI/Bettmann, Ron Vesley and Wide World Photos

Copyright © 1992 Creative Education, Inc.
International copyrights reserved in all countries. No part of this book may be reproduced in any form without written permission from the publisher. Printed in the United States of America.

Library of Congress Cataloging-in-Publication Data

Rambeck, Richard.

    Boston Red Sox / by Richard Rambeck.

    p. cm.

    Summary: A history of the team begun in 1901 under the name Boston Pilgrims.

    ISBN 0-88682-450-8

    1. Boston Red Sox (Baseball team)—History—Juvenile literature. [1. Boston Red Sox (Baseball team)—History. 2. Baseball—History.] I. Title.

GV875.B62R36 1991   91-2481

796.357'64'0974461—dc20   CIP

THE EARLY YEARS

The city of Boston is known as "The Hub"—short for "The Hub of the Universe"—because it boasts some of this country's best schools, libraries, and museums. Boston, the capital of Massachusetts, was also a hub of activity during the Revolutionary War.

The activity began in 1770, when British soldiers fired into a Boston mob and killed five people. In 1773 a group of colonists was so upset at what it considered to be unfair taxation by the British that it threw containers of tea off a British ship into Boston Harbor. This became known as the Boston Tea Party. Two years later Paul Revere rode his horse through the Boston area in the middle of the night to alert colonists that the British were on their way to destroy the colonists' weapon supply.

Pitcher Cy Young—in an unfamiliar pose.

Behind the pitching of Cy Young the Pilgrims won their very first game, defeating Philadelphia, 12–4.

Clearly Boston is a city rich in history and tradition, and part of that tradition is a professional baseball team known as the Boston Red Sox, a club that began playing in 1901. The Boston team, originally known as the Pilgrims, was one of the charter members of the American League. The Pilgrims were an immediate success, finishing second in the American League in 1901, third in 1902, and then winning the championship in 1903. Boston then defeated the National League winners, the Pittsburgh Pirates, five games to three to become the champion of professional baseball. In 1904 the team nickname was changed to the Red Sox, because of the color of the socks the club's players wore.

The early Boston teams were built around great pitchers, the most famous of whom was Denton "Cy" Young. He joined Boston in 1901 when he was thirty-three years old and pitched eleven years for the team. During his remarkable career, which included eleven seasons in the National League with St. Louis, Young won 511 games, easily the most ever by a pitcher and a record that may stand forever (no other pitcher has even won four hundred games). He had an amazing fourteen straight seasons with twenty or more victories. Young retired before World War I, but his name is still well known because each year the best pitcher in the American and National leagues is given the Cy Young Award.

Cy Young was the best-known Boston pitcher in the early years, but he wasn't the team's only great hurler. Big Bill Dinneen, Tom Hughes, and Jesse Tannehill each won more than twenty games at least once. Then, in 1908, a new pitching star joined the Red Sox. His name

Up against Boston's famed Green Monster.

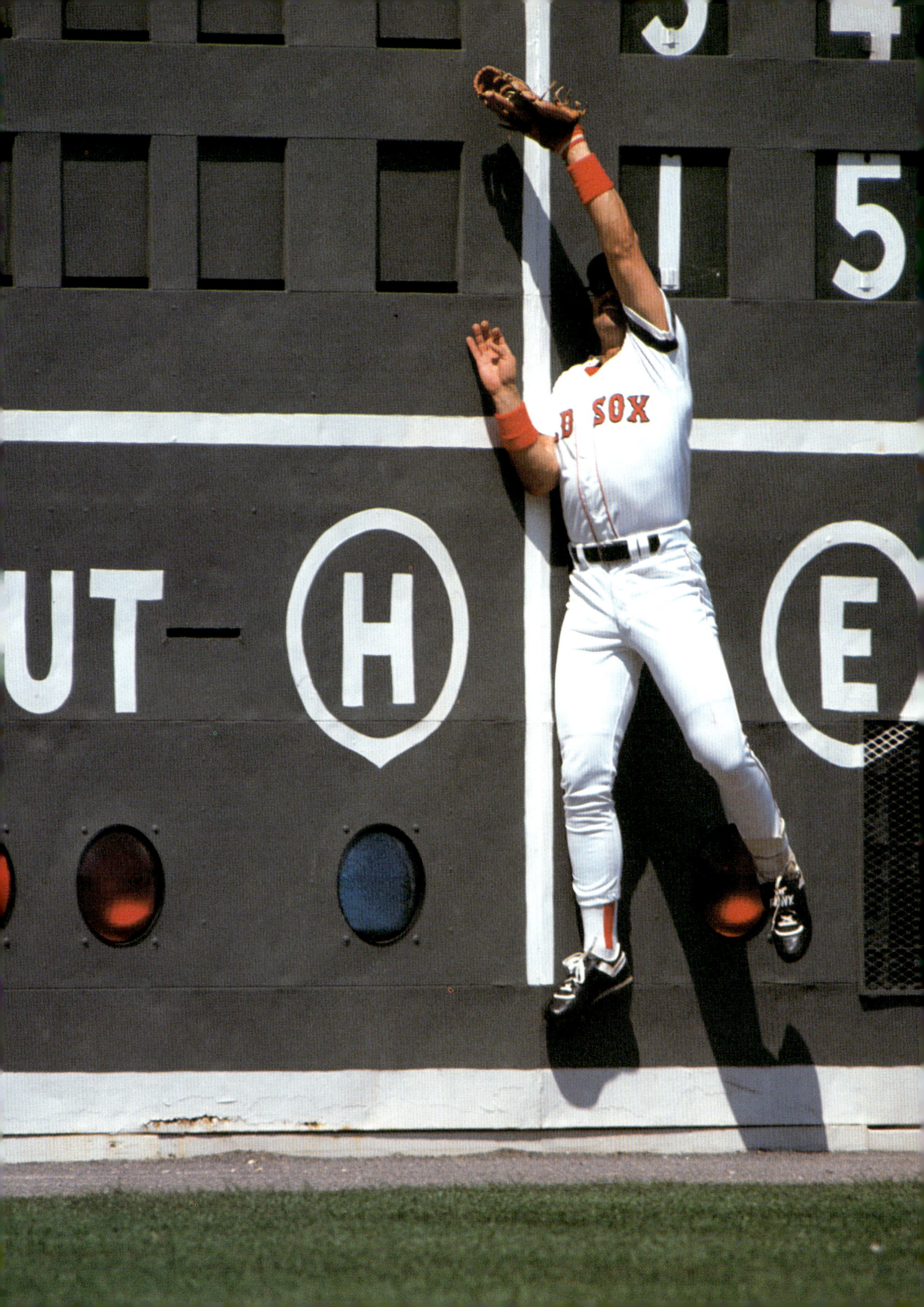

1
5
UT
H
E
SOX

Fenway Park opens. The stadium was named as such because it was located in the Fenway section of Boston.

was "Smokey Joe" Wood. He won twenty-three games in 1911 and then posted an incredible 34–5 record in 1912, leading the Red Sox to the American League pennant.

The Red Sox won the AL championship in their first season in Fenway Park, which replaced the team's Huntington Avenue Grounds in 1912. Fenway Park remains the home field of the Red Sox to this day. The team celebrated its first season in Fenway in grand style, beating the National League champion New York Giants four games to three in the World Series. The Red Sox didn't stop there. They won World Series titles in 1915, 1916, and 1918. Again, pitching was the key, and the team had a new star: George Herman Ruth, better known as "Babe." Ruth pitched sixteen scoreless innings in the 1916 series and thirteen more scoreless innings in the 1918 Fall Classic.

After the 1918 World Series, Ruth asked Boston owner Harry Frazee to switch him to the outfield so he could concentrate more on hitting. Frazee initially refused Ruth's request, but outfielder Harry Hooper talked Frazee into giving Ruth a chance. Ruth moved to the outfield, but soon, sadly, most of the Boston stars, including Ruth, moved to other teams.

Frazee, who bought the Red Sox in 1916, made a habit of selling star players to the New York Yankees to support his financially troubled Frazee Theatre in New York, located near the Yankees' office. The list of Red Sox stars Frazee sold to the Yankees is a long one, and it was topped by Babe Ruth. Thanks partly to Frazee, the Yankees built a dynasty, becoming the dominant team in the American League. The Red Sox, however, fell into a slump that lasted nearly twenty years. In fact, from 1919 to 1937, Boston never finished higher than fourth in the American League. In nine of those years, the once-mighty Red Sox finished last.

WILLIAMS IS AN IMMEDIATE HIT

Things started to improve for the Red Sox after Thomas Austin Yawkey bought the team in 1933. Yawkey's ownership style was the opposite of Frazee's. Frazee sold players; Yawkey bought them. Yawkey's first major acquisition was the Farrell brothers, catcher Rick and pitcher Wes. Yawkey then bartered with the Philadelphia Athletics of the National League and came away with two future Hall-of-Famers: pitcher Lefty Grove and slugger Jimmie Foxx. Yawkey then shocked other American League owners by spending $250,000 to bring Washington Nationals star Joe Cronin to the Red Sox organization. Cronin came as a player, but later became the team's manager.

Jimmie Foxx launched a Boston club record 50 home runs during the season.

While Yawkey was buying players, the Red Sox were also developing homegrown stars such as Bobby Doerr, Johnny Pesky, Dom DiMaggio, and a skinny outfielder named Ted Williams. Williams joined the Red Sox in 1939. The Red Sox veterans looked at the six-foot-three, 145-pound Williams and shook their heads. They almost laughed out loud when they saw him run the bases; Williams, with his bouncing gallop, looked like he was skipping rope.

Williams was awkward, but he was also very confident. "All I want out of life," he said when he made the major leagues, "is that when I walk down the street,

Another Boston great, Dwight Evans.

Future Hall of Famer Wade Boggs.

1 9 4 0

For the first time in his outstanding career second baseman Bobby Doerr (right) drove in over 100 runs.

folks will say, 'There goes the greatest hitter who ever lived.'" The other Red Sox noticed his confidence and kidded the rookie at every opportunity. "Wait'll you see Foxx hit, kid," one of them said to Williams, and Williams replied, "Wait until Foxx sees me hit."

It didn't take Williams long to become a star, and one of the best hitters in the American League. In 1941, only his third season in the big leagues, he hit an amazing .400 for most of the year. Coming into the last day of the regular season, his average was exactly .400. Williams could have not played in the season-ending doubleheader and preserved his .400 average, but the man they called "The Kid" would have none of that. "I don't want anyone ever saying that I made my .400 batting average by hiding in the dugout," Williams said. He played both games of the doubleheader, going six for eight to finish with a .406 average. It remains the last time a major-league player has hit .400 or better in a season.

Despite the heroics of Williams and other stars, the Red Sox didn't win a pennant until the 1946 season. That was the year all the Red Sox stars were reunited after several of them, including Williams, served their country in World War II. The Red Sox blended good hitting, always a team trademark, with solid pitching, led by Dave "Boo" Ferriss, to win 104 games and claim the American League title. In the World Series, though, the Red Sox lost to the St. Louis Cardinals four games to three. The Boston fans had waited twenty-eight years to cheer for an American League champion. Unfortunately, after 1946, they would have to wait twenty-one more years for the next pennant winner.

Ted Williams was named the AL Most Valuable Player as he led the Red Sox to the pennant.

After the success of 1946, the Red Sox slumped to third in the American League in 1947, followed by two second-place finishes in 1948 and 1949. The Red Sox fans started to get frustrated, and they took out much of their frustration on Williams, even though he led the American League in homers in 1947 and 1949, and won the batting championship in 1947 and 1948. In addition, Williams won the Triple Crown in 1947 by leading the league in homers, batting average, and runs batted in. (He also won the Triple Crown in 1942.)

Despite Williams's outstanding play, he was booed in Boston almost as much as he was cheered. The fans had high expectations for the team, and they were disappointed when the Red Sox and Williams couldn't win pennants. Between 1950 and 1966, the Red Sox never finished higher than third in the American League. Williams, though, continued to star for the team

Lefthanded ace Mel Parnell blanked the White Sox, 4–0, on his way to a no-hitter.

throughout the 1950s. In all, Williams won six American League batting titles, the last in 1958. Two years later he decided to retire, but not before hitting a memorable home run in Fenway Park in his last at-bat.

When Williams bid farewell to the Boston fans after hitting his homer, they stood and gave him a long standing ovation. Even though many of them had booed Williams during his career, all of them knew how special he was. Many of the fans wondered if Boston would ever have another player like Williams again. Then, just a year later, in 1961, Boston had a new left fielder, a player some were calling the next Ted Williams. That player was Carl Yastrzemski.

YAZ JAZZES UP THE SOX

Yastrzemski, who was known as "Yaz," wasn't a clone of Ted Williams. Yaz wasn't as tall, and he didn't have Williams's strength or power, but he did have a smooth swing. Like Williams, Yaz won an American League batting title in only his third year in major-league baseball, in 1963. Yaz was one of the top hitters in the American League almost every year; however, the Red Sox still weren't one of the top teams. Actually, they were among the worst—at least until 1967.

Despite the presence of Yastrzemski and several new young stars—outfielder Tony Conigliaro, first baseman George Scott, and pitcher Jim Lonborg—the Red Sox slumped to ninth in the ten-team American League in 1966. A year later, though, everything fell into place for the Red Sox and young manager Dick Williams. Conigliaro and Scott hit for power, although Conigliaro's

Aggressive play is a Boston tradition.

1 9 5 9

For the sixteenth time outfielder Ted Williams (right) was selected to the All-Star Game.

season would be cut short in August after he was hit in the eye with a blazing fastball. Lonborg became the first Red Sox hurler to win the American League's Cy Young Award, which was first given in 1956. But nobody had a better year than Yaz, who became the first American Leaguer in eleven years to win the Triple Crown.

"I remember saying to my wife," Yastrzemski said, "that if we sat down every day and planned situations in which I could be the hero, at bat and on the field, we couldn't have come closer than what actually happened." Yaz was the hero all season for the Red Sox, who won the American League pennant on the final day of the regular season with a victory over Minnesota.

For the first time since 1946, the Red Sox were in the World Series. As in 1946, their opponent was St. Louis,

"Yaz"—Carl Yastrzemski.

Like Jim Lonborg, Bruce Hurst was a great pitcher.

1 9 6 9

The young and talented Carlton Fisk (right) joined the Red Sox for the first time.

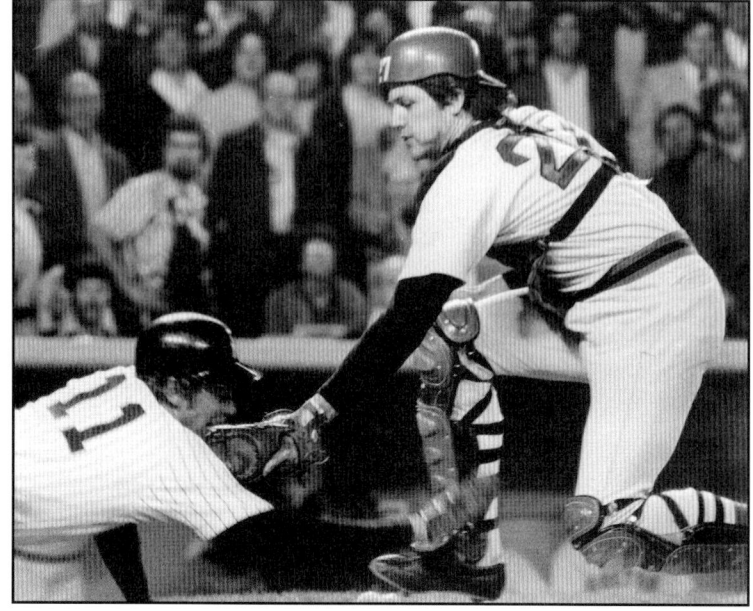

and also as in 1946, Boston lost four games to three, dropping the seventh game of the series in front of the screaming fans at Fenway Park. Despite their disappointment, the fans cheered loudly for the Red Sox after the game ended. They were cheering for a remarkable team that had gone from second-to-last to American League champs in one year.

The Red Sox weren't able to duplicate that great year again until 1975. Yastrzemski, though, was still a star, winning the 1968 American League batting crown. Sadly, Tony Conigliaro, who actually was leading the American League in home runs in 1967 before his terrible eye injury, never regained the form that made him one of the brightest young stars in baseball. Additionally, Jim Lonborg never had another year to compare with his Cy Young season of 1967.

The Red Sox, however, built a stable of new stars. Catcher Carlton Fisk won the Rookie of the Year Award in the American League in 1972. Three years later, the Red Sox added two more rookies—Fred Lynn and Jim Rice—who turned the club from a merely good one into a pennant contender. During the 1975 season, Rice wound up hitting .309 with twenty-two home runs and 102 RBI. Center fielder Lynn had an even better year; he batted .331, and was named both Rookie of the Year and Most Valuable Player in the American League.

Led by Lynn, Rice, Fisk, and pitcher Luis Tiant, the Red Sox won the East Division of the American League in 1975. (The AL was divided into two divisions in 1969—the East and the West.) Boston then defeated AL West champion Oakland three games to none to claim the American League pennant and advance to the World Series. The Red Sox had to play in the Fall Classic without Rice, who broke his wrist late in the season. Despite this handicap, Boston still gave National League champion Cincinnati fits. Five of the seven games in the series were decided by one run, including both the sixth and seventh games.

The Red Sox trailed in the series three games to two before the sixth game, which was played in Boston. In that game, Boston overcame a Cincinnati lead and eventually won by a score of 7–6 on a homer by Fisk in the twelfth inning. In the seventh game, Cincinnati broke a 3–3 tie with a run in the top of the ninth, and went on to win the game and the series.

Two years later, the Red Sox battled the New York Yankees down to the last day of the regular season for the AL East crown. The two teams wound up tied for first

Luis Aparicio joined Carl Yastrzemski, Carlton Fisk and Reggie Smith on the AL All-Star team.

Second baseman Marty Barrett.

and had to meet each other in a one-game playoff at Fenway Park. Boston fans were shocked when New York shortstop Bucky Dent, the most unlikely of power hitters, slammed a home run that buried the Red Sox and sent the Yankees into the American League Championship Series.

After 23 seasons with the Red Sox Carl Yastrzemski retired with a career batting average of .285.

It was to be the last chance for Carl Yastrzemski to play on a pennant-winning team. Yaz, who retired after the 1983 season, became the only American Leaguer ever to hit at least four hundred home runs and accumulate at least three thousand base hits. Not even Babe Ruth, Mickey Mantle, Joe DiMaggio, Ty Cobb or Ted Williams was able to do what Yastrzemski did. "He's a true superstar," said Reggie Jackson, another player who could be called a superstar. "You really have to have other athletes comment on what he has achieved, because you can't really appreciate what it means to perform as he has for as long as he has."

Frank Robinson, another superstar, was equally impressed by Yastrzemski. "It's a great accomplishment to blend power with consistency," said Robinson, who is fourth on the all-time home run list with 586. "When I was playing in the league, he was the only one I considered a true superstar." When Yastrzemski retired, the Red Sox already had a new young hitter with superstar potential ready to follow in the footsteps of Ted Williams and Yaz. His name was Wade Boggs.

WADE'S WOOD PROVES TO BE A WINNER

When Boggs, a third baseman, joined the team in the early 1980s, the Red Sox already had a player

24　　　*Left to right: Mike Greenwell, Marty Barrett, Roger Clemens, Jim Rice.*

in that position, Carney Lansford, who was an excellent hitter. Lansford had won the 1981 American League batting title. But everybody knew Boggs was also a great hitter, so the Red Sox decided to trade Lansford and give Boggs a shot at starting. He didn't disappoint the team. In 1983, his first full year as a starter, Boggs won the league batting title. In fact, Boggs won five batting titles in six years between 1983 and 1988.

For the second time in three years Wade Boggs led the AL in hitting; batting an incredible .368.

What makes Boggs such a good hitter? Two things stand out: his concentration and his preparation. When batting, Boggs concentrates so hard on the pitcher, he goes into a trancelike state he calls a "cocoon." "When I'm in the cocoon," Boggs said, "I can eliminate distractions and variables and shut out the entire world except for me and the pitcher. I don't like surprises. I face enough of the unexpected when I'm hitting. I don't need any others."

Boggs also meditates before games. "I like to focus in on who's pitching, what he, the catcher, the manager, and the defense are likely to try to do with me.... It's nothing more than preparation."

Boggs and other strong hitters such as Jim Rice, Dwight Evans, and Marty Barrett gave the Red Sox one of the best offenses in baseball. But Boston's pitching wasn't good enough for the team to contend for a pennant. It wasn't, that is, until 1986, when a tall right-hander from Texas named Roger Clemens moved to center stage.

THE ROCKET TAKES OFF

Before the 1986 season, Clemens was a hard thrower who had control problems. He walked too many

Wade Boggs (pages 26–27).

In his second year as manager John McNamara led the Bosox to the AL pennant.

batters, and that kept him from becoming a consistent member of Boston's starting rotation. But in 1986 something was different; Clemens had improved a lot, and it was obvious from the beginning of the season. On April 29 Clemens and the Red Sox faced the Seattle Mariners at Fenway Park. That night he threw a three-hitter as Boston won 3–1, but that wasn't the biggest story. Clemens struck out twenty Mariners, setting a major-league record for strikeouts in a game by one pitcher. And amazingly, Clemens didn't walk a single batter. "I can always show my kid that I was part of something that hadn't happened before and might not happen again," said Seattle slugger Gorman Thomas, who homered for the Mariners' only run.

Suddenly, Clemens, nicknamed "The Rocket," was unbeatable; he won fourteen games in a row during the 1986 season. "He's accomplishing history," said Boston pitcher Al Nipper, "and it's fun having the locker next to his, watching him and talking to him about it. Heck, the Red Sox went from 1980 to 1985 without a starting pitcher winning fourteen games, and he's won fourteen in a row."

Clemens finished the 1986 season with a 24–4 record, which was good enough to win him the Cy Young Award. But perhaps Clemens' most important contribution to the Red Sox was establishing respect for the pitching staff. "Anyone who had been around the Red Sox over the years knew that pitchers were considered second-class citizens," said Bruce Hurst, another Boston pitcher. "It was always the pitcher's fault that the Red Sox lost. That all has changed, and it changed because of Roger."

1 9 8 6

Bill Buckner (left), will always be remembered for a not so great moment in the World Series.

Clemens led the Red Sox to the AL East title in 1986. Boston then beat California four games to three in a thrilling American League Championship Series. Unfortunately, Boston's luck ran out in the World Series against the New York Mets. The Red Sox won three of the first five games and took a 5–3 lead into the bottom of the tenth inning of game six. All they needed were three outs to claim a world championship. The first two outs came easily, but Boston never got the third one. The Mets suddenly exploded for hit after hit after hit, finally winning the game when a grounder went through Boston first baseman Bill Buckner's legs. New York won game six 6–5 and then took game seven, and the series, with an 8–5 victory.

Despite this devastating loss, the Red Sox rebounded and remained one of the top teams in the American

Pitcher Roger Clemens.

Center fielder Ellis Burks.

1991

Led by center fielder Ellis Burks the Red Sox were one of the AL's best teams.

League. Led by the pitching of Clemens and Hurst, and the hitting of Boggs, Rice, and newcomers Mike Greenwell and Ellis Burks, Boston won the AL East in 1988. However, the Red Sox were swept by the Oakland A's in the league championship series.

The Red Sox used gutty performances by several key players to capture another American League East title in 1990. "I've been on lots of Red Sox teams with more talent than this one," Dwight Evans said during the 1990 season, "but never one with more character." The team's title run was keyed by the veteran leadership of Clemens, catcher Tony Pena, and pitcher Mike Boddicker. Youngsters such as Burks and first baseman Carlos Quintana provided the spark that lifted Boston to the top of the division.

As the 1990s began, the Red Sox had some of the best talent in baseball. Boggs is perhaps the game's best hitter. Clemens is considered by many to be the top pitcher in the major leagues. Burks is rapidly becoming one of the most feared hitters in the American League.

Thanks to these stars, Boston fans have high hopes for a World Series championship, something the Red Sox have not claimed since 1918. They've been so close, so many times, losing in seven games in 1946, 1967, 1975, and 1986. Amazingly, Boston stars such as Ted Williams, Jimmie Foxx, Joe Cronin, and Carl Yastrzemski never played on a World Series winner for Boston. Many experts believe it's only a matter of time before the current team ends more than seventy years of disappointment and claims a World Series title.